CD #1: See next page for track listing.

D1479164

Track Listing for CD #1:

CHANTING FOR DEEP MEDITATION

With

SRI DURGA MATA

Selections from Paramahansa
Yogananda's *Cosmic Chants*,
and reminiscences of his life
and teachings,
by one of his early close disciples

Self-Realization Fellowship
FOUNDED 1920
Paramahansa Yogananda

Authorized by the International Publications Council of Self-Realization Fellowship

The Self-Realization Fellowship name and emblem (shown above) appear on all SRF books, recordings, and other publications, assuring the reader that a work originates with the society established by Paramahansa Yogananda and faithfully conveys his teachings.

ISBN-13: 978-0-87612-460-4
ISBN-10: 0-87612-460-0

Printed in the United States of America

2049-J2640

CONTENTS

Sri Durga Mata, around 1935, on the grounds of Self-Realization Fellowship International Headquarters, Mount Washington, Los Angeles

Preface

The year 2013 marks the 110th anniversary of the birth of Sri Durga Mata (November 8, 1903), as well as the 20th anniversary of her passing (January 16, 1993). It is with loving memories of this beloved soul that Self-Realization Fellowship offers this book and the accompanying audio discs to commemorate her contribution to the work of Paramahansa Yogananda.*

Sri Durga Mata was one of the early close disciples of Paramahansa Yogananda, and played a unique role in the establishment of his worldwide work. Along with others of the great Master's "first generation" of disciples, Durga Mata was privileged to serve him personally for many years and to absorb the spirit of devotional chanting from him firsthand.

The genesis of this book was a request from Sri Daya Mata, revered president and spiritual head of Self-Realization Fellowship from 1955 until her passing in 2010. Daya Mata and Durga Mata had both spent decades as part of the inner circle of Paramahansaji's close disciples; Daya Mata's loving memories of those years are included in this book (see page 7). Several years before her passing, Daya Mata directed the monks and nuns in SRF's Publications and Audio Departments to gather a representative selection of the archival recordings of Durga Mata playing Paramahansaji's devotional chants for deep meditation, restore them as well as possible, and make them available for others. Sri Daya Mata followed the progress of this project until her passing on November 30, 2010, and we are sure she would be deeply pleased that it has now been completed in time to commemorate Durga Mata's anniversaries mentioned above.

Self-Realization Fellowship
December 2012

---

* Founder of Self-Realization Fellowship / Yogoda Satsanga Society of India and author of *Autobiography of a Yogi*. (See page 61, "About Paramahansa Yogananda.")

5

Sri Durga Mata (November 8, 1903 – January 16, 1993)

Memorial Tribute to Sri Durga Mata

By Sri Daya Mata

Durga Mata passed away at the Self-Realization Fellowship International Headquarters (the Mother Center) on January 16, 1993. On January 21, Self-Realization Fellowship President Sri Daya Mata paid tribute to Durga Mata in a memorial service, which was printed in the Spring 1993 issue of Self-Realization *magazine:*

The night before our beloved Durga Mata left this world, I went to see her. Sitting by her bed, I observed that she had gone into a deep state of consciousness. Her face was illumined with such a loving expression, such peace. It was evident that she would not remain with us much longer. She passed away, very peacefully, early the next morning.

Durga Mata was born November 8, 1903, in Iron Mountain, Michigan. She met Paramahansa Yogananda in November 1927, and entered the ashram here at Mt. Washington on December 15, 1929.*

There is so much that could be said about our dear Durga Mata. There were just a handful of us disciples here in those early years. Being two of the younger ones, Durga Ma and I formed a bond that lasted throughout our lives. She was the elder, and I

---

* Her name before joining the ashram was Florina Darling. As a renunciant of the monastic order of Self-Realization Fellowship, she was known as "Durga Mata" or "Durga Ma"—the name given to her by Paramahansaji. "Durga" is an Indian name of the Divine Mother; "Ma" or "Mata" means "mother."

will be eternally grateful for the loving, mothering concern she expressed toward me. I was a very young girl when I came here to seek God; it was an inspiration to watch her, to follow her example. How I treasure the memory of those years—the early mornings when a group of us disciples would go to her room to meditate when Guruji was absent on lecture tours. She would lead us, in her sweet voice, in chanting to the Divine. Those were days of great devotion, days that lifted our consciousness on high.

Durga Mata dedicated her entire life to service in Master's work, and many were the responsibilities he placed upon her. In the spirit of discipleship, she served in a wide variety of capacities, including rendering personal service to Gurudeva—cooking for him and cleaning his living quarters.

One of the assignments Guruji gave Durga Ma was to work on his housecar. He had acquired the body, but it needed a chassis.* So Guruji bought a secondhand chassis that had been part of a Dodge truck. When it was brought to the ashram, he gave Durga Ma the responsibility of uniting that housecar with its new chassis. We were in awe, because it seemed an impossible task! But he knew that anything he asked of her, she would find a way to accomplish.

I remember the first time we undertook a refurbishing of the

---

* The housecar was reputedly built by the Pullman Company. It was equipped with electric lights, gas cooking, expanding beds, and bathroom with shower—a forerunner of the recreational vehicles that became popular decades later. Paramahansaji enjoyed traveling in the housecar, often taking small groups of disciples on outings to wilderness areas for meditation.

Opposite: Paramahansa Yogananda (center) at the SRF Encinitas Hermitage, 1937, with four of his closest disciples: (from left) Durga Mata, Rajarsi Janakananda (James J. Lynn), Daya Mata, Ananda Mata.

Administration Building here at Mt. Washington. Durga Ma tied a rope around herself and climbed all over the building, painting and doing whatever else she could to repair it. How Master appreciated that "can-do" spirit!

Guruji knew he could rely on Durga Ma to carry out his wishes in anything having to do with architectural matters or designing of buildings. In the early 1930s, he acquired a temple on Seventeenth Street here in Los Angeles, and Durga Ma was given the assignment of renovating it. Guruji gave services there for a number of years.*

While Master was in India in 1935–36, Durga Ma played a very important role in the construction of the Hermitage in Encinitas. Years before, she and I had been among a small group of disciples who travelled with Guruji to a certain area overlooking the ocean at Encinitas; in those days it was called Noonan's Point. We sat on the bluff top meditating and chanting, and enjoyed a picnic lunch. Guruji talked about how beautiful this spot was; he loved it very much. After he went to India, some of us accompanied Durga Ma and Rajarsi Janakananda† to Encinitas, and Rajarsi decided to purchase the site and build a hermitage there—a place where Guruji could come for retreat and to work on his writings. Rajarsi entrusted Durga Ma with the responsibility of supervising the designing and furnishing of that beautiful

---

* The temple property was later taken over by the city of Los Angeles for a freeway right-of-way.

† An exalted disciple of Paramahansa Yogananda, and his first spiritual successor as president of Self-Realization Fellowship/Yogoda Satsanga Society of India. A wealthy businessman from Kansas City, he was known as James J. Lynn before receiving from Paramahansaji the monastic title and name of Rajarsi Janakananda in 1951. Out of regard for Mr. Lynn's spiritual advancement, the Guru referred to him as "Saint Lynn." See also page 23.

hermitage. When Master returned from India, what a blessed sur-
prise it was for him when he saw for the first time the new ashram
on the site he had visited many years before.

In later years, when Rajarsi began to spend more and more
time at Mt. Washington and Encinitas, Guruji gave Durga Ma the
assignment of looking after this beloved disciple. With what care
she attended to Rajarsi's needs; with what care she carried mes-
sages back and forth between Rajarsi and Master when they didn't
have an opportunity to meet. She actively served Rajarsi until his
passing in 1955, as Gurudeva wished her to do.

In the late 1930s, Guruji decided to build a Golden Lotus
Temple in Encinitas, adjacent to the Hermitage grounds. Again,
Durga Ma's expertise was called upon. She worked with Gurudeva
on the designing of the temple, and later with the building contrac-
tor during construction.*

A few years later, someone told him about a little wooden
chapel that was for sale in the San Fernando Valley. He went
to see it and immediately purchased it and had it transported
to Hollywood. Durga Ma had the responsibility of carrying out
Guruji's wishes for transforming that building into the beautiful
temple we have today. She personally did all of the gold-leaf work
decorating the temple. With devotion and enthusiasm, she went
every day to oversee the renovation. A year later she served in the
same way at the SRF temple in San Diego. She had such a sense
of beauty and balance, which was expressed in everything she did
for Guruji's work.

Durga Ma was a faithful servant of Guruji through all those
years. She served in positions of great importance to his work. In

---

* In 1942, erosion of the bluffs caused the temple to slip its foundations, and
it had to be dismantled.

Sri Daya Mata, president of Self-Realization Fellowship from 1955 to 2010, with several of the close early disciples of Paramahansa Yogananda: (left to right) Uma Mata, Sahaja Mata, Ananda Mata, Durga Mata, Mrinalini Mata, Sri Daya Mata; Brothers Anandamoy, Bhaktananda, Mokshananda, Premamoy.

early 1935, under Gurudeva's guidance, she met with lawyers to have Self-Realization Fellowship legally incorporated. She was a Director of Self-Realization Fellowship from 1935, appointed by Gurudeva for a lifelong term, and served first as Treasurer and later as Secretary. During Guruji's stay in India, Durga Ma, along with Gyanamata, was given the responsibility of supervising the activities of the work here in America. They were a wonderful combination—Durga Ma with her devoted, capable spirit in looking after the work, and our blessed Gyanamata with her wise, loving counsel, which was sought by us all.

As a member of the Board of Yogoda Satsanga Society of India, Durga Mata visited India on three different occasions. Here at Mt. Washington she held *satsangas* and served the many, many devotees who came to seek her counsel and understanding.

In 1986 Durga Ma determined that it was necessary for her to resign from the Board of Directors for reasons of health. Her years of faithful dedication, loyalty, and service to our revered Guru and his great work of Self-Realization Fellowship/Yogoda Satsanga Society of India had earned the profound love and respect of all who had served with her, and of SRF/YSS members worldwide. Though honoring her wish to retire, we told her that we would continue to appreciate whatever contributions her health would permit her to make to the discussions of the Board regarding the guidance and furtherance of the work of our Gurudeva.

To the very end, Durga Ma's mind was firmly fixed on the one love of her life, God; and on dedication to her Guru's work. So many benefited from her counsel, her classes, her teaching. In her we had a wonderful example of sincerity, forthrightness, truthfulness, love, and courage. She was truly one of Master's great disciples.

Right: Durga Mata on the grounds of Yogoda Math (headquarters of Yogoda Satsanga Society of India), on the banks of the Ganges River, Dakshineswar, West Bengal, during one of her three trips to India.

Below: Durga Mata and companions during trip to India.

Bottom: Durga Mata and Sailasuta Mata, another longtime monastic disciple of Paramahansa Yogananda, who accompanied Durga Mata on her first trip to India.

Let me read from a letter Master sent her, for I can think of no greater tribute to Durga Ma than these words he wrote to her from India. Durga Ma did not have a great deal of schooling—that is not important; it doesn't mean a thing in the sight of the Divine—but she had a great deal of wisdom and understanding. Master refers to this in his letter to her of June 24, 1936:

> Dear Durga,
>
> I know not when I have been as pleased with anyone, next to Saint Lynn. Among my men disciples Mr. Lynn has the first seat in heaven and in my heart. And among my lady disciples, you will have the first seat with Sister [Gyanamata] in heaven and in my consciousness. Your behavior and work has pleased me most. And how could an uneducated one like you become so educated in everything? I have been the same way in life: read very little, but written much. Are you flattered? No. But all this I say—what comes from within—for the most wonderful cooperation which you have given....
> Meditate and dedicate yourself to God, and behave best before yourself within, and before all.
>
> Ever yours. SY

I cannot say enough about this beloved soul. I treasure her love, as all of you do who knew her. She had a vast ocean of love within her. Guruji once said to me, "If you touch her heart, you will feel the great love that flows from Durga Mata."

In paying tribute to her, let me share with you this thought from *The Imitation of Christ:* "Jesus hath many lovers of his heavenly kingdom, but few bearers of his cross. He hath many desirous of his consolation but few of his tribulation. He findeth many companions of his table but few of his abstinence. All desire to rejoice in him, but few are willing to endure anything for him or with him. Many follow Jesus into the breaking of bread, but few to the drinking of the cup of his passion. Many reverence his miracles, but few followed him to his cross. Many love Jesus, so long as no adversities befall them."

Durga Ma was one of those who followed Master loyally and steadfastly through all of the trials, burdens, and heartaches he went through in starting this work. She joins those other angelic souls, now departed, who came in the early years to help in establishing this society, which nourishes our souls and feeds us with the teachings of Paramahansa Yogananda. For that, she has a fitting place at the feet of our blessed Gurudeva.

May this occasion remind each of us of our own true nature, for we are not these physical forms; we are not these bodies; rather, we are immortal, we are blissful souls, made in the image of God. From Him we have come and back to Him each one of us will one day go again. Our dear Durga Mata has been released from all physical limitations to enjoy a greater freedom in Spirit.

Remember that those loved ones who have gone before us can receive, and benefit from, our loving thoughts. So as we think of Durga Ma at this time, let it not be with sorrow, but with great joy. For she will receive the vibrations of friendship, goodwill, and divine love. May the blessings of God ever encompass her, and draw each one of us to the realization of our oneness, our unity, in God.

Opposite: Durga Mata in front of Self-Realization Fellowship International Headquarters atop Mount Washington, Los Angeles. At this fifteen-acre hilltop ashram founded by Paramahansa Yogananda in 1925, Durga Mata dedicated her life to seeking and serving God from 1929 until her passing in 1993 — more than sixty years of discipleship on the path of Kriya Yoga meditation.

Chanting for Deep Meditation

By Sri Durga Mata

Durga Mata often met with groups of devotees in the Self-Realization Fellowship ashrams to share the personal training she received from Paramahansa Yogananda about the art of spiritual chanting. These gatherings provided an opportunity not only for the disciples to learn the Master's chants,* but also the art of chanting with concentration, understanding, and devotion. Following is a compilation of her comments on these occasions.

The Spiritual Power of Devotional Chanting

Chanting, Master used to tell us, is one of the ways of realizing God. It is a powerful method of focusing the mind on one point. When you concentrate deeply on the words of the chant and the thought that is being expressed as you chant to God, your mind goes deeper and deeper into actual perception of God.

Chanting is a wonderful way to prepare the mind for practice of the yoga meditation techniques taught by Master. Chanting is preparation for deep meditation, an encouragement; the real communion is in silent meditation.

It is another form of prayer—a constant repetition of a prayer.

---

* Paramahansa Yogananda is respectfully addressed by his disciples as "Guruji" or "Master"—a master of himself. Though the word *guru* is often misused to refer simply to any teacher or instructor, a true God-illumined guru is one who, in his attainment of self-mastery, has realized his identity with the omnipresent Spirit. Such a one is uniquely qualified to lead the seeker on his or her inward journey toward divine realization.

When you really feel what you are singing, it becomes a prayer, because everything that you feel deeply is a prayer.

Chanting is a loud prayer, but its purpose is to take us beyond music and words into the deep stillness of silent meditation. That is why when we chant, we try to control the mind and concentrate it one-pointedly on the thought expressed in the words of the chant. Then when the chanting is over, we are more easily able to go into silent meditation, beyond manifestations of thought, chanting, voices, or anything. That is the only time God can come: in the calmness and interior stillness of mind.

Chanting is a method to help us calm and interiorize the mind. When our minds are restless—flitting back and forth, here and there, with one distraction after another—it's like taking a glass of muddy water, as Master used to say, and continuing to stir it so that it stays muddy. But if you let it sit still for a while, you will see that the mud settles to the bottom and you have clear water on the top. So chanting is a method to help us settle the muddy sediment of restlessness and psychological debris, so that we can clearly perceive Truth, or God.

Experiencing the Divine Presence

[*Durga Mata and other disciples were privileged to accompany the Guru on occasional outings to wilderness areas for chanting and deep meditation. She often described one such occasion when meeting with devotees for chanting and meditation:*]

I remember once when Master went to Palm Canyon, in the desert

Opposite: Durga Mata was part of a small group who went with Paramahansaji to Los Angeles' Laurel Canyon (an undeveloped natural area at the time) on New Year's Day, 1930, where these photos of Paramahansaji were taken.

near Palm Springs, with a group of devotees. We went down into that
canyon and meditated; and Master went into a very deep *samadhi*.

I wasn't near him; I was meditating on a rock alone. After
some time, he called us all together to return to the housecar. As
he walked along the path through the canyon, I was close behind
him. Suddenly I felt a tremendous stillness emanating from him.
It wasn't from within me; it was coming from him. I was close
enough to be in the aura of his vibrations. Immediately it lifted
me into a state of deep, transcendent stillness.

I continued walking, and was conscious of everything around
me—seeing the stones in the path that I had to step over—and yet
I wasn't feeling my body at all. There was only this feeling of omnipresent stillness; I was not conscious that I was in the body at all.

Then Master turned around to me and said: "Pick up some
wood." We had to make a fire. I got my load of wood and walked
with my load of wood—but didn't lose one single bit of that bliss-
filled stillness. My mind was calm and still—there was no ripple
of restlessness or thought, and yet I could see and feel everything.
When we reached the housecar, I put down the wood I was carrying, and then he turned to me and said: "Stillness is God."

It was a great lesson. We are made in the image of God; and
as Master used to say: "God is right here, right within us. Why
don't you see Him? Because you are looking everywhere else."
You can find Him today, tomorrow, anytime, as long as you turn
your consciousness within and hold it within, and not constantly
throw it outside.

Calmness: Mark of a Real Yogi

Master used to say that because he was very strong-willed himself, he would attract strong-willed people.

People who have a strong will are very energetic. That is

because their energy is thrown out into the limbs, into activity. When we practice Kriya Yoga, we try to reverse that and throw it within instead of all without.* Master was very energetic; but yet he was very, very calm. He acted calmly. Of course, he could talk very loudly if he wanted to; his voice was strong because he could throw that energy into his voice. But he was always calm—never restless. He knew how to withdraw that energy within. And when he wanted to accomplish something, he could throw it outward into energetic activity.

Master used to say that a yogi is the opposite of a restless man. A restless man remains constantly in motion—move, move, move, all the time. If you try to make him sit quietly for five minutes, he'll still fidget and move around—restless!

That's one thing that Rajarsi was cured of the first time he ever met Master.† Like an ordinary businessman, he threw all his energies outside, moving restlessly all the time. But the minute Master interiorized those energies—without him knowing it—the first thing he knew he was sitting there, and he looked down on his body and said: "What's happened to me? I'm not moving around." Master healed him instantaneously of that. And he never was restless after that.

"A yogi," Master says, "is calm all the time, and when he has to act, then he can act quickly." Master was quick when he wanted

---

* Kriya Yoga is a sacred spiritual science, originating millenniums ago in India. It includes certain techniques of meditation whose devoted practice leads to realization of God. It is taught to qualified students of the *Self-Realization Fellowship Lessons*. See page 66.

† His biography, including more than seventy pages of Paramahansa Yogananda's personal letters to him, is published by Self-Realization Fellowship: *Rajarsi Janakananda: A Great Western Yogi —The Life of Paramahansa Yogananda's First Spiritual Successor.*

With Rajarsi Janakananda in the Encinitas Hermitage, 1954.

to do something—very quick. But when he was finished, he was back to his calmness again. So that's how we all have to act. Be calm all the time. When you have to perform some action or duty, you put your energies forward; and then when you finish, you interiorize your will again. That is being a yogi—a real yogi!

The Benefits of "Spiritualized" Chants

When Master went into a deep period of *samadhi,* he often came out with a new chant, giving expression in words to what he had perceived—as he did with his chant "Mother, I Give You

My Soul Call," which he composed after a deep meditation in Palm Canyon.*

When Master composed these chants, he used to repeat them over and over again until, as he said, they would become "spiritualized." What he meant was that he chanted them repeatedly until he had realized through actual experience the spiritual perception behind every word that he put into these chants. He chanted them not with just his voice, but with his heart and mind and especially his soul. And when we chanted with him, if we really threw ourselves into the chanting, his spiritualized perceptions overflowed from his consciousness into our own, giving us a glimpse of the wondrous blissful communion he was experiencing.

Master's words are so inspiring and so deep. Just tune in with them as you chant. As Master used to say, "Those who tune in more, receive more." So when you chant, do so with feeling, and you will receive what he found when he chanted.

Some of his chants are sorrowful, full of yearning—the devotee's heartfelt appeal to God to remove the veil that hides His presence. Some of them are joyous chants, and some are chants

---

* Paramahansa Yogananda related this experience in *Man's Eternal Quest* twice, in the chapters titled "Is God a Father or a Mother?" and "The Purpose of Life Is to Find God."

He said: "I had just finished the song when I saw a wondrous form, the Divine Mother! appear from out of the sky. In response to my soul call, I beheld everywhere, in everything, the Cosmic Mother. I prayed and worshiped Her. She blessed me and talked with me."

"God has no form, but to please a devotee He can take any form that devotee desires. You have no idea how wonderful the Divine Mother is; how great She is; how loving She is!

"There is no greater experience than to feel and know that the Cosmic Mother is with you. Watch for the presence of the Mother, because She will look after you in every way."

that take our consciousness into the spine. Master says that it is through the spine that we have to reach God; for the spine and the brain are the altar of God. This you experience through the practice of Kriya Yoga—you go within the spine to the altar of God, and there you find the Infinite.*

Intensifying the Heart's Yearning for God

[One chant that Durga Mata found particularly poignant was "Divine Love's Sorrow." She spoke about this on various occasions in satsangas *with devotees:]*

I remember when in 1930 Master wrote this song, "Divine Love's Sorrow." He wrote it as a song, and also a little differently as a chant; but he wrote the song first. He was sitting at the kitchen table in the big dining room here at Mt. Washington. Somebody had brought a record of Fritz Kreisler's "Liebesleid"—"Love's Sorrow"—and was playing it on the phonograph for Master. And it struck his heart. Master always put a spiritual interpretation to everything, so he made "Love's Sorrow" into "Divine Love's Sorrow." He had one of the disciples hum the melody while he was composing words for it. I can just hear him saying: "Hum it again! Hum it again!" The poor thing, it seemed she would have to hum all day long! But he worked on the words, and then he put the words together with the song, and finally he had it. And once he had the words set to Kreisler's melody, then he made part

---

* Paramahansa Yogananda explained that as the consciousness in man awakens through practice of the yoga science of meditation (taught in his *Self-Realization Fellowship Lessons*), it disconnects itself from the senses and moves upward through the *chakras*, or centers of light and superconsciousness in the spine to the altar of Spirit in the "thousand-petaled lotus" in the brain, where one communes in ecstasy with the indwelling presence of God.

of that song into a more Indian-sounding chant, which was easier than the Western music for him to play on the harmonium.

It has beautiful words. Usually he would ask me to sing that song at the all-day Christmas meditations. And I remember when we went to Palm Canyon, he had me sing it amidst those centuries-old trees and ancient rock formations in that canyon. Then it really penetrated, what he meant: "Centuries and centuries, through endless incarnations, I called out Thy Name." We feel that yearning when we sing it with all our heart and mind.

See God in Every Moment

If you think now, at this moment, that you are one with God—and you actually feel that oneness with God, and nothing else around you matters—that's realizing God, isn't it? Now, if you could just hold that thought all the time, whether you're working or whatever you are doing! Then if you are thinking, you know that the thought comes from God. When you are speaking, you know that the words come from God. When you are working, you feel that the energy comes from God.

You can see God in every moment. You can feel God in every thought that you think. The only thing necessary is to change your mind from worry to God, that's all. We've trained our minds to worry about this, that, and the other thing! Now you have to train it to be calm so that worry doesn't disturb you—so that you are able to do something about it, but not let it disturb you. Thoughts and worries will come, but it's not that you should keep them there; it's not that you should give them a "welcome home"!

It's simple, but you have to train your mind in that way. You see how you can make yourself happy or unhappy by just changing your thoughts, your consciousness. And by changing your consciousness, you can contact God—by keeping your mind calm.

If your mind is calm, you won't be disturbed. And when something comes to disturb it, if it is a problem you can solve, your calmness will bring your intuition to solve that problem. A disturbed mind never solves anything—never! In fact, it prevents you from solving anything. A calm mind solves everything. But it is through calmness that it solves the problem, not by being ruffled about it. And by the same token, when you say that God is so far away, all you have to do is make Him close, and there you have Him. So it's all in the mind. And your practice of Kriya and the other meditation techniques is to quicken and purify your thoughts, so that you may be able to think this way all the time.

Guarding the Happiness You Feel in Meditation

God is ever-existing, ever-conscious, ever-new bliss. When you can get that ever-new bliss within yourself, you are one with God.

God is happiness. Being made in His image, we have that happiness and bliss within ourselves—all we have to do is regain that happiness through meditation. And once you regain that happiness, guard it with your life; jealously guard that happiness! To do so, you have to make a shield. Your mind has to be the shield to protect your feelings from being hurt, to protect you from getting into moods. If you protect yourself in this way, you can be always with God.

When you feel joy and bliss in meditation, that *is* God. Then why in the world do we allow little things to come along to disrupt it? If we are working hard to meditate and to practice our Kriya, why shouldn't we work as hard to protect the happiness it brings?

Safeguard your bliss. Safeguard your joy. When you feel even the slightest little bit of joy inside, try to increase that joy by not losing it, by not letting anybody or anything come between you and that little spark of joy—because that little spark of joy is a spark of God.

About the enclosed audio recordings...

Setting and Quality of the Recordings

These renditions of Paramahansa Yogananda's Cosmic Chants, performed by Sri Durga Mata, were recorded at various times in the 1950s through the early 1970s—most of them during informal gatherings at Self-Realization Fellowship headquarters. (A few were made during her visit to the ashram of Yogoda Satsanga Society of India at Ranchi.)

Though the equipment used on these occasions reflects the simple ashram setting of many decades ago, far removed from the professional conditions of a recording studio, these chants have a personal quality of focused devotion and meditative concentration that gives them a special power and appeal. Now digitally restored for the first time, they are offered here in tribute to the memory of this beloved disciple of Paramahansa Yogananda—one who absorbed the art and spirit of yogic chanting directly from the great master during many years of personal association with him.

Spoken Comments in Addition to the Chants

As mentioned earlier, Durga Mata often met with groups of devotees for *satsanga* (meditation and spiritual inspiration). Her custom at these gatherings was to say a few words about the spiritual life, or read selections from Paramahansa Yogananda's lectures,* and then lead the group in chanting followed by meditation. Often she would preface the chants with some comments about

---

* Three volumes of Paramahansa Yogananda's Collected Talks and Essays have been published by Self-Realization Fellowship thus far: *Man's Eternal Quest, The Divine Romance, and Journey to Self-Realization.*

the meaning of the chant, or about the way to chant for maximum spiritual benefits. In addition to the chants, the enclosed CDs include nine tracks of spoken comments of this nature.

Instrumentation Used in the Chants

On all the chants (except the song "Divine Love's Sorrow," as noted below), Durga Mata sings and plays the harmonium (a small, hand-pumped reed organ often used in Indian-style chanting).

On one of the chants (CD #1, track 11), Durga Mata is accompanied by devotees playing drums, bells, and cymbals—*kirtan*-style.

On "Divine Love's Sorrow" (CD #1, track 14), Durga Mata's singing is accompanied by the melody played on organ by Dr. M. W. Lewis, a much-loved early disciple of Paramahansa Yogananda and former vice-president of Self-Realization Fellowship.*

Variations in Melody and Phrasing

Paramahansa Yogananda would sometimes introduce slight variations in the wording and melodies of his chants when he performed them extemporaneously, expressing some new inspiration he was feeling at the moment. His book *Cosmic Chants* (published by Self-Realization Fellowship) gives the versions that are most representative and were most often played by him. As one of Paramahansaji's early close disciples, Durga Mata heard him sing these chants many times over the years, including his variants of them. In later years, after the Guru's passing, Durga Mata was

---

* See *Dr. M. W. Lewis: The Life Story of One of the Earliest American Disciples of Paramahansa Yogananda*, published by Self-Realization Fellowship, which includes a biography and several lectures he gave in the SRF temples during his years as a beloved minister of SRF.

part of a committee of disciples who reviewed the various versions of the chants and finalized the "standard" rendition to be published in *Cosmic Chants,* so that the chants could more easily be learned and sung in unison by congregations in Self-Realization Fellowship temples, centers, and meditation groups.

Some of Durga Mata's renditions on the enclosed CDs reflect the above-mentioned variations and are therefore slightly different in melody, rhythm, and phrasing from the more typical versions of the chants published in *Cosmic Chants* and sung in SRF meditation services. The book *Cosmic Chants* is the best source for those wishing to learn to play these chants themselves. However, Durga Mata's feeling of devotion and her intense concentration on the spiritual meaning of the chants—abundantly evident on all of these recordings—beautifully exemplifies the *spirit* of chanting for deep meditation.

Durga Mata grew up in a French-Canadian family, and her speech retained a distinctive accent to some degree throughout her life. This can be heard in her pronunciation and phrasing in some of the chants.

Technique of Chanting

In many of the chants, Durga Mata gradually decreases the volume of her singing at the end, to lead the devotees into periods of silent, mental chanting followed by deep meditation, as taught by Paramahansa Yogananda.

The Guru speaks of this aspect of the technique of chanting in *Cosmic Chants:* "Progress from low voice to loud, then loud to whisper, and lastly from whisper to mental chanting, until you feel that you are repeating the words and music with soul feeling—that is, until you finally realize the meaning of your

Durga Mata in the early 1930s, playing the mridanga *(a drum used for accompanying* kirtan *chanting in India) at Self-Realization Fellowship International Headquarters.*

utterance in every fiber of your being. The devotional thought in a song should be predominant, while the sound of the words meekly, gently follows the increasingly warm feeling of love for the Lord."

Selections from 1970 SRF World Convocation

On the second CD, the last eleven tracks were recorded by SRF monks at the 1970 Self-Realization Fellowship World Convocation. These selections also include the voices of the large audience, who had come from all over the world for the Convocation, and who chanted along with Durga Mata during

the special class on chanting and long meditation that she con-
ducted. This class was held in the Music Room of the Biltmore
Hotel in Los Angeles, where Paramahansa Yogananda entered
mahasamadhi in 1952.

Final thoughts on chanting, from *Cosmic Chants*...

The importance and power of the habit of devotional chanting cannot be overestimated. To banish inertia, indifference, lack
of devotion, sad moods, blind attachments, and a host of other
enemies of spiritual enlightenment, "chanting is half the battle,"
said the great master, Paramahansa Yogananda. Chanting opens
for the devotee a way through which the joyous presence of God
can be felt.

Paramahansaji said: "One who sings these spiritualized songs,
Cosmic Chants, with true devotion will find God-communion
and ecstatic joy, and through them the healing of body, mind,
and soul....

"Each of these chants should be sung not once but many
times, utilizing the cumulative power of repetition, until the sing-
er feels great bliss wafting through the "radio" of his heart....

"He who chants these songs with great devotion, in solitude
or in congregational singing, will later discover that the chants
are repeating themselves in the subconscious background of his
mind, bringing an ineffable joy even while he is in the thick of
the daily battle of activity."

Durga Mata in her apartment on the fourth floor of the SRF Mother Center, where for many years she welcomed SRF devotees for meditation, chanting, and personal counsel.

Lyrics and Notes for the Chants

The words and music of the chants on the enclosed CDs, unless otherwise noted, are original compositions by Paramahansa Yogananda, or are translations of Sanskrit, Hindi, or Bengali songs in original adaptations by Paramahansaji.

Durga Mata's explanatory words are given on the tracks marked "Spoken comments." Notes in brackets have been added by Self-Realization Fellowship, primarily from the book *Cosmic Chants* by Paramahansa Yogananda.

As is customary in devotional chanting, Durga Mata repeats various lines of the chants as an aid in deepening one's concentration on the meaning. Not all of her repetitions of lines are shown in the lyrics printed here.

CD #1 Contents

Track 1: Opening prayer

Heavenly Father, I am the prince of peace, sitting on the throne of poise, directing the kingdom of activity.

Om Peace, Om Joy, Om Bliss. Amen.

Track 2: Opal Flame

If thou wilt see opal flame, drive darkness evermore,
Searing thy silence with the sword of *pranayam.*

Through the star in opal eye, see the Christ everywhere,
Sleeping in every atom, in protons, electrons.

Golden, misty aureole adorns the opal door;
Through the star in the blue, meet the Christ everywhere.

Starry dove with wings of rays alights on forehead,
Showing you the throne of Christ in the peace of every heart.

Make thine eyes a single flame to see the starry gate;
Thy body will be Light, illumining all space.

By wise inspiration, follow the starry eye,
To see the Christ born in thy soul anew.

Starry dove with wings of flame, baptize me in thy Light,
Spreading my soul with Christ in the bliss everywhere.

Starry opening in hall of matter, through thee I peep through*
Into the land of astral light that kindles life in everything.

If thou wilt see opal flame, drive darkness evermore.

[This chant describes the devotee's passage through the "door" of the spiritual eye within the forehead. The yogi beholds the spiritual eye as an aureole of golden light encircling a sphere of opalescent blue; and at the center, a brilliant white star. (Paramahansaji explained that when Jesus was baptized by John the Baptist, he saw the starry spiritual eye as "Spirit descending from heaven like a dove." Its "wings" represent the halos of blue and gold rays.) Those who by devotion and *pranayama* techniques (such as Kriya Yoga) pass through the starry door commune with the Christ Consciousness that permeates all creation.]

---

* A variant rendering. The more common wording of this line is, "Shining opening in hall of matter, O star! I peep through thee"— referring to the silvery white star in the center of the spiritual eye.

Track 3 (spoken comments): "See God in Every Moment"
(See also page 27.)

Track 4: Search Him Out in Secret

Without meditation, mind,
Hither, thither wanderest thou.
Without meditation, mind,
Hither, thither wanderest thou.
Adorable Him! Adorable Him!
Search Him out in secret now.
Search Him out in secret now.

Floating on the breeze of bliss,
In the chariot of sky,
Peering into His eyes
With thy diving eye.

Thousand petals' nectar drink!
Drink and drink, drink!
With cosmic mighty Om,
Deeper do thou sink.

[The "diving eye" is the spiritual eye or center of Christ Intelligence in man, within the forehead between the eyebrows. With its spherical vision the deeply meditating yogi beholds the beautiful inner world of the astral plane.

The "thousand-petaled lotus," or *sahasrara,* is a subtle astral center of divine consciousness in the cerebrum, where in the highest states of meditation oneness with the Infinite is experienced. When the devotee is transfixed in *samadhi,* an astral nectar flows from the thousand-petaled lotus, purifying the devotee's body and filling him with bliss. Throughout this experience, he hears the all-pervasive sound of *Om* (the creative manifestation of God as cosmic intelligent vibration—see sidebar on page 52).]

Track 5: I Will Be Thine Always

My Lord, I will be Thine always.

I may go far, farther than the stars,
But I will be Thine always.
My Lord, I will be Thine always.

Devotees may come, devotees may go,
But I will be Thine always.
My Lord, I will be Thine always.

When I die, look into mine eyes;
They will mutely say, "I have been Thine always."
My Lord, I will be Thine always.

Track 6 (spoken comments): "Calmness: Mark of a Real Yogi"
(See also page 22.)

Track 7: Learn Thou Self-Control

O my mind! learn thou self-control.
Go not in the house of senses;
Learn thou self-control.

Track 8: In the Land Beyond My Dreams

In the land beyond my dreams,
Where no clouds come, and golden dreams dwell,
I sit by life's well,
In the land beyond my dreams.

Heart to heart meeting, Spirit and soul's greeting,
In the land beyond my dreams.

The ark is waiting, and I am dreaming,
Of the land beyond my dreams.

In the ark of silence, silently we go,
To the land beyond my dreams.

> ["This earth is full of imperfection; but in the Land Beautiful
> no clouds come and we can materialize the golden dreams
> of our earth sojourn. Only the ark of silence can take us to
> that Land. There all hearts meet in unity and wisdom; our
> love is not limited by human attachment, for our souls greet
> the Spirit in one another. If only you would take the ark of
> silence, you would reach that Land where you all want to
> go." —Paramahansa Yogananda]

Track 9 (spoken comments): "On Chanting"

Track 10: Do Not Dry the Ocean of My Love

Do not dry the ocean of my love
With the fires of my desires,
With the fires of my restlessness.

For Thee I cry, for Thee I weep.
I'll cry no more, for Thou art mine evermore.

Thee I find
Behind the fringe of my mind.
Hide no more, Lord, hide no more.
Leave me not, Lord, leave me not.

Track 11: O Thou Blue Sky / Paramahansa Yogananda, Jai Guru, Jai

O thou blue sky, under blue cover
Hast thou hidden my beloved Lord?

[Repeat]

Open thy cover, let me discover
My beloved Lord in thy heart of hearts.

[Repeat]

Jai Guru, jai Guru, jai Guru, jai!

Jai Guru, jai Guru, jai Guru, jai!
Paramahansa Yogananda, jai Guru, jai!
Paramahansa Yogananda, jai Guru, jai!

["Jai Guru" means "Hail to the Guru" or "Victory to the Guru."]

❖   ❖   ❖

Track 12: Spoken comments on "Divine Love's Sorrow"
(See also page 26.)

❖   ❖   ❖

Track 13: Divine Love's Sorrow
(Chant version, played on harmonium. Words and music by Paramahansa Yogananda.)

I have been roaming,
Forsaken by Thee,
Who hast seen me groping,
Hardly ever answering.
I shall be roaming, I shall be roaming,
Bursting all boundaries of heart;
Ever more moving towards Thee,
To Thy vast unthrobbing heart.

Through endless incarnations I called out Thy Name,
Through endless incarnations I called out Thy Name,
Searching by the streamlets
Of all my silvery dreams.

Track 14: Divine Love's Sorrow
(Song version; organ played by Dr. M. W. Lewis. Words by Paramahansa Yogananda, sung to the tune of Fritz Kreisler's "Liebesleid.")

I have been roaming,
Forsaken by Thee,
Who hast seen me groping,
Hardly ever answering.
I shall be roaming,
Bursting all boundaries of heart;
Ever more moving towards Thee,
To Thy vast unthrobbing heart.

Come Thou to me, O Lord!
Oh, come at last to me!
Centuries and centuries,
I have waited now for Thee.
Through endless incarnations
I called out Thy Name,
Searching by the streamlets
Of all my silvery dreams.

I knew that Thou must come at last
To steal the flowers of my heart.
In sorrow-thrills I piped my love,
I sadly sang my song to Thee.
And yet I knew my love must reach Thee,
Though many lives I had to wait.
On mountain crags of high devotion
I sadly sang my song, my song.

❖ ❖ ❖

Track 15: Spoken comments on "Desire, My Great Enemy"

❖   ❖   ❖

Track 16: Desire, My Great Enemy

Desire, my great enemy, with his soldiers surrounded me;
Is giving me lots of trouble, oh, my Lord!

That enemy I will deceive, remaining in the castle of peace,
Night and day in Thy joy, oh, my Lord!

What will be my fate?
O Lord, tell me.

"*Pranayam* be thy religion, *pranayam* will give thee salvation.
Pranayam is the wishing tree.
Pranayam is beloved God, *pranayam* is Creator-Lord.
Pranayam is the Cosmic World.

"Control the little *pranayam*,
Become All-Pervading Pranayam.
You won't have to fear anything anymore."

[Paramahansa Yogananda said: "We often used to chant this
song at Sri Yukteswarji's hermitage in Bengal, long ago. The
devotee asks the Lord how to overcome man's greatest enemy,
Desire. God replies that the best way to outwit the adversary
is through use of the inner yoga technique of *pranayama* (lit.,
'control of *prana* or life force'). Lahiri Mahasaya gave the sacred *pranayama* or Kriya Yoga technique to the world again,
after it had been covered through priestly secrecy and man's
indifference with the dust of many centuries. Practice of this
technique enables man to gain control of his inner life force

and thus realize his oneness with the Cosmic Life Force. With poetic license, the composer of this song calls the Lord Himself 'Pranayama' even though, strictly speaking, He is not identical with any method or technique. Yet of all the ways of reaching Him, *pranayama* is the quickest and most holy."]

Track 17: Spoken comments on "Why, O Mind, Wanderest Thou?"

Track 18: Why, O Mind, Wanderest Thou?

Why, O mind, wanderest thou?
Go in thy inner home!

On the left, *ida*; on the right, *pingala*.
In the middle, the taintless *sushumna*.
Seize, seize her with all thy might!

Kundalini power in the subtle form
Liveth unconscious in the coccyx region.
Guru-given power by *pranayama* wake,
Wake her with all thy might!

Guru-given power by Kriya wake,
Wake her with all thy might!

[The "inner home" of the mind is the spine and brain. The yogi must cultivate an unwavering mind to be able to enter the holy astral channel of the *sushumna* in the spine and to ascend through the various centers of life and consciousness to the highest center of God-realization in the brain. *Ida* and *pingala* are two astral currents of life force that entwine the astral spine. *Kundalini*, as explained by Paramahansaji, "is the coiled current at the base of the spine, a tremendous dynamo of life that when directed outward sustains the physical body and its sensory consciousness; and when consciously directed upward, opens the wonders of the astral cerebrospinal centers." It is said to be "asleep" or "unconscious" in the unenlightened human being, and "awakened" by long and successful practice of guru-given techniques of *pranayama* meditation.]

Track 19: Wink Has Not Touched My Eyes
(Here Durga Mata sings one of Paramahansaji's variant renderings: "Wink did not touch my eyes...." The wording more frequently used by Paramahansaji was, "Wink has not touched my eyes...." which is the version printed in *Cosmic Chants* and familiar to most devotees.)

Wink did not touch my eyes ever since I saw Thee.
Without Thee, my breath does not want to flow.
Wink did not touch my eyes ever since I saw Thee.
Thou didst say Thou would come, but Thou didst not come.
Restless is my soul, day and night.

CD #2 Contents

Track 1 (spoken comments): "Guarding the Happiness You Feel in Meditation"
(See also page 28.)

❖   ❖   ❖

Track 2: Who Is in My Temple?
(Words by Rabindranath Tagore. Music by Paramahansa Yogananda.)

Who is in my temple?
All the doors do open themselves,
All the lights do light themselves.
Darkness, like a dark bird,
Flies away, O flies away.

[The "doors" spoken of here correspond to the spinal *chakras*—astral centers of light, consciousness, and energy sometimes called "lotuses" because of their petal-like outer filaments. Ordinarily these petals hang downward, but when the consciousness of the deeply meditating yogi enters the spine and begins its marvelous ascent through each *chakra* to the higher centers in the brain, the petal-doors turn upward or "open" themselves. Each *chakra* is characterized by a distinctive light, sound, and state of consciousness. The intuitive divine realizations bestowed on the yogi as he passes through these spinal doors drive away from the body temple the "dark bird" of spiritual ignorance.]

❖   ❖   ❖

Track 3: In Samadhi

In *sabikalpa samadhi yoga*, you will drown yourself in your Self.
In *nirbikalpa samadhi yoga*, you will find yourself in your Self.

[In *sabikalpa samadhi yoga*, you will drown (melt) your self (ego) in your Self (Spirit). In *nirbikalpa samadhi yoga*, you will find (see) your self (ego) in your Self (Spirit).

In *sabikalpa samadhi* the devotee attains temporary realization of his oneness with Spirit but cannot maintain his cosmic consciousness except in the immobile trance state. By continuous meditation he reaches the higher state of *nirbikalpa samadhi*, in which he may move freely in the world and perform his outward duties without any loss of God-perception. He realizes fully his identity as Spirit.]

Track 4: Come, Listen to My Soul Song

Come, listen to my soul song,
Soul, soul, soul, soul song,

Burst the heart, burst the blue,
Burst the heart, burst the blue, burst the soul!

Come, listen to my soul song,
Soul, soul, soul, soul song.

Hovering over the clouds, lingering over the lea,
Hovering over the clouds, lingering over the lea,
Thou hast come to listen to my soul song.
Soul, soul, soul, soul song.

Track 5: Receive Me on Thy Lap, O Mother

Receive me on Thy lap, O Mother!
Cast me not at death's door.

Receive me on Thy lap, O Mother!
Cast me not at delusion's door.

❖   ❖   ❖

Track 6 (spoken comments): "Experiencing the Divine Presence"
(See also page 20.)

❖   ❖   ❖

Track 7: Sitting in the Silence
(Words by Paramahansa Yogananda, sung to the melody of
"Roaming in the Gloaming" by Sir Harry Lauder.)

Sitting in the silence on the sunny banks of my mind;
Sitting in the silence with the Krishna by my side.
When the thoughts have gone to rest,
That's the time I see him best,
Oh, 'tis lovely sitting in the silence.

Sitting in the silence on the sunny banks of my mind;
Sitting in the silence with the Christ by my side.
When the thoughts have gone to rest,
That's the time I see him best,
Oh, 'tis blissful sitting in the silence.

Track 8: I Am Om

I am Om, I am Om.
Om, Om, I am Om.
Om, Om, I am Om.

Omnipresence, I am Om.
All-Blessed, I am Om.

Om, Om, come to me;
Come to me, oh come to me!

O my Jesus, come to me;
Come to me, oh come to me!

O my Krishna, come to me;
Come to me, oh come to me!

O my Babaji, come to me;
Come to me, oh come to me!

Om Lahiri Mahasaya, come to me;
Come to me, oh come to me!

Sri Yukteswar, come to me;
Come to me, oh come to me!

O my Guru, come to me;
Come to me, oh come to me!

O my Mother, come to me;
Come to me, oh come to me!

Divine Mother, come to me;
Come to me, oh come to me!

I am Om, I am Om.
I am Om, I am Om.

Om, Om, Om.

OM (Aum): SANSKRIT WORD-SYMBOL FOR GOD
(Explanation from *Cosmic Chants*)

Devotees should end all periods of meditation or chanting by intoning *Om* as is done at the end of this chant, "I Am Om."

The chanting of *Om* (*Aum*), from which the word *Amen* derives, is similar to the practice in Western churches of intoning *Amen* one or more times at the conclusion of a hymn.

Aum is the basis of all sounds. The *Aum* of the Vedas became the sacred word *Hum* of the Tibetans; *Amin* of the Moslems; and *Amen* of the Egyptians, Greeks, Romans, Jews, and Christians. *Amen* in Hebrew means *sure, faithful*. *Aum* is the all-pervading sound emanating from the Holy Ghost (Invisible Cosmic Vibration; God in His aspect of Creator); the "Word" of the Bible; the voice of creation, testifying to the Divine Presence in every atom. *Aum* may be heard through practice of Self-Realization Fellowship methods of meditation.

"These things saith the Amen, the faithful and true witness, the beginning of the creation of God" (Revelation 3:14).

The great Hindu sage Patanjali said: "He who knows *Om*

knows God." Chant *Om* in the following manner, while meditating on the threefold nature of creation: its causal aspect, or vibratory manifestation as an idea of God; its astral aspect, or vibratory manifestation as light and energy; and its physical aspect, the objective manifestation of causal and astral vibrations.

Intone the first *Om* with full voice, concentrating on the physical creation as epitomized in the human physical body; the second *Om,* representing the astral or electronic sphere of creation, should be sung more softly, with thought concentrated on the astral creation as epitomized in the electrical energies in the human body; the third *Om,* representing the causal sphere of creation, should be sung quite softly, with the mind interiorized on the causal creation epitomized in man's own power of creative thought.

Repeat the chant again and again with deep attention and devotion. Always try to listen for the real *Om* sound, which is an astral vibration and is only symbolized in the vocal sound of *Om* that you are chanting.

The chant "I Am Om," which Durga Mata sings here, also invokes the blessings of Jesus Christ and Bhagavan Krishna, as well as the other Gurus of Self-Realization Fellowship: Mahavatar Babaji, Lahiri Mahasaya, Swami Sri Yukteswar, and Paramahansa Yogananda (the last being the direct guru of all Kriya Yoga members of SRF/YSS). The lives of these modern-day masters are described in *Autobiography of a Yogi* (see page 62 of this booklet).

Tracks 9–19: Durga Mata leading long meditation with chanting during the 1970 SRF Convocation, at the Biltmore Hotel, Los Angeles, July 9, 1970

Track 9: Opening prayer

Heavenly Father, Mother, Friend, Beloved God, Jesus Christ, Bhagavan Krishna, Babaji, Lahiri Mahasaya, Sri Yukteswarji, and our beloved Guruji, Paramahansa Yoganandaji, saints of all religions, we bow to You all.

Heavenly Father, I will reason, I will will, I will act, but guide Thou my reason, will, and activity to the right thing that I should do in everything.

Om Peace, Om Joy, Om Bliss.

❖ ❖ ❖

Track 10 (spoken comments): "The Art of Devotional Chanting"

❖ ❖ ❖

Track 11: Learn Thou Self-Control

O my mind! learn thou self-control.
Go not in the house of senses;
Learn thou self-control.

Opposite: *In the Biltmore Hotel, Los Angeles, at the 1970 Self-Realization Fellowship World Convocation, where Durga Mata led a class on "The Art of Devotional Chanting." The class was held in the Music Room of the Biltmore (photo on page 57), the room where, on March 7, 1952, Paramahansa Yogananda had entered* mahasamadhi *(a great yogi's conscious exit from the body at the time of physical death).*

Track 12: Thou Art My Life
(Words and music by Rabindranath Tagore)

Thou art my life, Thou art my love,
Thou art the sweetness which I do seek.

In the thought by my love brought,
I taste Thy Name, so sweet, so sweet.

Devotee knows how sweet You are.
He knows, whom You let know.

Track 13: My Krishna Is Blue

My Krishna is blue, the *tamal* tree is blue;
So I do love thee, *tamal* tree!
So I do love thee, my *tamal* tree!

And when I die, O Mother!
Do put me high
On a branch of the *tamal* tree.

Where Krishna sat, there I would die,
On a branch of the *tamal* tree.

[This chant refers to a legend that Bhagavan Krishna left his
body while seated in a blue-blossomed *tamal* tree.]

Music Room of the Biltmore Hotel during the 1970 SRF Convocation. Here Durga Mata led chanting and meditation for the many who attended from all over the world.

"The entire 2½ hours was electric," recalls one devotee who was there. "Even the hotel people stood in the back and listened. And during the meditations in between each period of chanting, there was a profound stillness and joy that permeated the gathering." Recordings from this event are included on CD #2, enclosed.

Track 14: O Thou Blue Sky

O thou blue sky, under blue cover
Hast thou hidden my beloved Lord?
Open thy cover, let me discover
My beloved Lord, in thy heart of hearts.

Track 15: I Am the Bubble, Make Me the Sea

So do Thou, my Lord:
Thou and I, never apart.
Wave of the sea, dissolve in the sea!
I am the bubble, make me the sea,
Make me the sea, oh, make me the sea!

Track 16: Door of My Heart

Door of my heart, open wide I keep for Thee.*
Wilt Thou come, wilt Thou come?
Just for once, come to me?
Will my days fly away
Without seeing Thee, my Lord?
Night and day (oh) night and day,
I look for Thee night and day.

[Devotees in Calcutta, India, love to recall occasions in 1935 when Paramahansa Yogananda sang this song, repeating the line "Wilt Thou come, just for once come to me" by the hour, sometimes late into the night, and dancing in a state of divine ecstasy, surrounded by inspired crowds of dancing devotees.

Paramahansaji said: "Your mind should continually whisper:

---

* On this chant Durga Mata sings "Open, I keep for Thee" instead of "Open wide I keep for Thee," reflecting a variant rendering of this chant that was in use for a time in the early years.

'Night and day I look for Thee, night and day.' That is the philosophy of life by which you should live."]

Track 17: Paramahansa Yogananda, Jai Guru, Jai / Om Chant
("Jai Guru" means "Hail to the Guru" or "Victory to the Guru.")

Jai Guru, jai Guru, jai Guru, jai!
Jai Guru, jai Guru, jai Guru, jai!
Paramahansa Yogananda, jai Guru, jai!
Paramahansa Yogananda, jai Guru, jai!

Track 18: Glory Hallelujah / Om Chant
(Adapted from "The Battle Hymn of the Republic" by Julia Ward Howe. Paramahansaji often sang the following words at the close of Sunday services at Self-Realization Fellowship temples and during the all-day Christmas meditations.)

In the beauty of the lilies Christ was born across the sea.
As he died to make men holy, let us live to make men free.
As he died to make men holy, let us live to make men free.
His love is marching on.

Glory, glory hallelujah!
Glory, glory hallelujah!
Glory, glory hallelujah!
His love is marching on.

Om, Om, Om.

Track 19: Closing prayer

Heavenly Father, Mother, Friend, Beloved God, Jesus Christ, Bhagavan Krishna, Babaji, Lahiri Mahasaya, Sri Yukteswarji, and our beloved Guruji, Paramahansa Yogananda, saints and sages of all religions, we bow to You all.

Heavenly Father, may Thy love shine forever on the sanctuary of our devotion, and may I be able to awaken Thy love in all true hearts.

Make my soul Thy temple, make my heart Thy altar, make my love Thy home.

Om Peace, Om Joy, Om Bliss.

About Paramahansa Yogananda

"The ideal of love for God and service to humanity found full expression in the life of Paramahansa Yogananda.... Though the major part of his life was spent outside India, still he takes his place among our great saints. His work continues to grow and shine ever more brightly, drawing people everywhere on the path of the pilgrimage of the Spirit."

In these words, the Government of India paid tribute to the founder of Self-Realization Fellowship/Yogoda Satsanga Society of India, upon issuing a commemorative stamp in his honor on March 7, 1977, the twenty-fifth anniversary of his passing.

Paramahansa Yogananda began his life's work in India in 1917 with the founding of a "how-to-live" school for boys, where modern educational methods were combined with yoga training and instruction in spiritual ideals. In 1920 he was invited to Boston as India's representative to an International Congress of Religious Liberals, and later that year he established Self-Realization Fellowship to disseminate his Kriya Yoga teachings. Subsequent lectures in Boston, New York, and Philadelphia were enthusiastically received, and in 1924 he embarked on cross-continental speaking tour.

For the next decade Paramahansaji traveled extensively, giving lectures and classes in which he instructed thousands of men and women in the yoga science of meditation and balanced spiritual living. In 1925 he established the Self-Realization Fellowship International Headquarters in Los Angeles, and from there the spiritual and humanitarian work he began continues today under the guidance of one of his foremost disciples, Sri Mrinalini Mata, president of Self-Realization

Fellowship. In addition to publishing Paramahansa Yogananda's writings, lectures, and informal talks (including a comprehensive series of lessons on the science of Kriya Yoga meditation), the society oversees Self-Realization Fellowship temples, retreats, and meditation centers around the world; monastic training programs; and a Worldwide Prayer Circle, which serves as a channel to help bring healing to those in need and greater peace and harmony among all nations.

Quincy Howe, Jr., Ph.D., Professor of Ancient Languages, Scripps College, wrote: "Paramahansa Yogananda brought to the West not only India's perennial promise of God-realization, but also a practical method by which spiritual aspirants from all walks of life may progress rapidly toward that goal. Originally appreciated in the West only on the most lofty and abstract levels, the spiritual legacy of India is now accessible as practice and experience to all who aspire to know God, not in the beyond, but in the here and now.... Yogananda has placed within the reach of all the most exalted methods of contemplation."

The life and teachings of Paramahansa Yogananda are described in his *Autobiography of a Yogi*, which has become a classic in its field since its publication in 1946 and is now used as a text and reference work in colleges and universities throughout the world.

Autobiography of a Yogi

"A rare account."   — The New York Times

"A fascinating and clearly annotated study."   — Newsweek

"There has been nothing before, written in English or in any other European language, like this presentation of Yoga."
                                    — Columbia University Press

"These pages reveal, with in comparable strength and clarity, a fascinating life, a personality of such unheard-of greatness, that from beginning to end the reader is left breathless. We must credit this book with the power to bring about a spiritual revolution."
                        — Schleswig-Holsteinische Tagespost, Germany

Additional Resources on the Kriya Yoga Teachings of Paramahansa Yogananda

Self-Realization Fellowship is dedicated to freely assisting seekers worldwide. For information regarding our annual series of public lectures and classes, meditation and inspirational services at our temples and centers around the world, a schedule of retreats, and other activities, we invite you to visit our website or contact our International Headquarters:

www.yogananda-srf.org

Self-Realization Fellowship
3880 San Rafael Avenue
Los Angeles, CA   90065-3219
(323) 225-2471

Also by Paramahansa Yogananda

Audio Recordings of Paramahansa Yogananda

- *Beholding the One in All*
- *Awake in the Cosmic Dream*
- *Songs of My Heart*
- *Be a Smile Millionaire*
- *The Great Light of God*
- *To Make Heaven on Earth*
- *One Life Versus Reincarnation*
- *Removing All Sorrow and Suffering*
- *In the Glory of the Spirit*
- *Follow the Path of Christ, Krishna, and the Masters*
- *Self-Realization: The Inner and the Outer Path*

Other Publications From Self-Realization Fellowship

The Holy Science by Swami Sri Yukteswar

Only Love: Living the Spiritual Life in a Changing World by Sri Daya Mata

Finding the Joy Within You: Personal Counsel for God-Centered Living by Sri Daya Mata

Enter the Quiet Heart: Creating a Loving Relationship With God by Sri Daya Mata

God Alone: The Life and Letters of a Saint by Sri Gyanamata

"Mejda": The Family and the Early Life of Paramahansa Yogananda by Sananda Lal Ghosh

Self-Realization (a quarterly magazine founded by Paramahansa Yogananda in 1925)

A complete catalog of books and audio/video recordings — including rare archival recordings of Paramahansa Yogananda — is available on request or online at www.yogananda-srf.org.

SELF-REALIZATION FELLOWSHIP
3880 San Rafael Avenue • Los Angeles, CA 90065-3219
TEL *(323) 225-2471* • FAX *(323) 225-5088*
www.yogananda-srf.org

Self-Realization Fellowship Lessons

Personal guidance and instruction from Paramahansa Yogananda on the techniques of yoga meditation and principles of spiritual living

If you feel drawn to the spiritual truths described in *Chanting for Deep Meditation With Sri Durga Mata*, we invite you to enroll in the *Self-Realization Fellowship Lessons.*

Paramahansa Yogananda originated this home-study series to provide sincere seekers the opportunity to learn and practice the ancient yoga meditation techniques that he brought to the West—including the science of *Kriya Yoga*. The *Lessons* also present his practical guidance for attaining balanced physical, mental, and spiritual well-being.

The *Self-Realization Fellowship Lessons* are available at a nominal fee (to cover printing and postage costs). All students are freely given personal guidance in their practice by Self-Realization Fellowship monks and nuns.

For more information...

Complete details about the *Self-Realization Fellowship Lessons* are included in the free booklet *Undreamed-of Possibilities.* To receive a copy of this booklet and an application form, please visit our website or contact our International Headquarters.

Other Recordings of Paramahansa Yogananda's Cosmic Chants

The Voice of Paramahansa Yogananda

- *Songs of My Heart:* Chants, Poems, and Prayers by Paramahansa Yogananda.

Other Chants and Kirtan

- *Light the Lamp of Thy Love:* Devotional chanting led by nuns of Self-Realization Fellowship.

- *I Will Sing Thy Name:* Devotional chanting led by monks of Self-Realization Fellowship.

- *I Will Be Thine Always:* Selections from *Cosmic Chants,* sung by nuns from the ashram of Paramahansa Yogananda.

- *When Thy Song Flows Through Me:* Monks from the ashrams of Paramahansa Yogananda sing selections from his *Cosmic Chants.*

- *When My Dream's Dream Is Done:* Devotional chanting led by nuns of Self-Realization Fellowship.

- *Mi corazon Te espera (Spanish):* Renditions in Spanish from Paramahansa Yogananda's *Cosmic Chants.*

Instrumental Arrangements

- *The Divine Gypsy*
- *Where Golden Dreams Dwell*
- *Thou Art My Life*
- *In the Land Beyond My Dreams:* Organ renditions of Paramahansa Yogananda's *Cosmic Chants.*